Park Güell :: Antoni Gaudí

Park Güell is a magical, enigmatic and symbolic place. Its creator, architect Antoni Gaudí, knew how to combine traditional techniques with new technology and transformed a rugged mountain into an avant-garde space. However, the park isn't just a magnificent exponent of early 20th century art and architecture, but also a great puzzle of symbols created by its architect in order to be deciphered. From the main entrance up to the top of the mountain, and in each of the constructions, Gaudí left behind a multitude of clues so that the ideals underlying Park Güell could be interpreted.

CONTENTS

01 | THE BIRTH OF A DREAM
The origins of the park

A utopian urban garden city project for the new industrial elite of the time.

Catalonia's rapid industrialisation towards the end of the 19th century led to great social change and the emergence of new movements removed from religion and tradition. The rupture of the old values urged the Catalan industrial elite, who was seeking a way to return to medieval hierarchical order, to embark on numerous initiatives to revive religious values and Catalan traditions. Within this context, Eusebi Güell, a powerful industrialist and promoter of the park, actively participated in this cultural revival movement, along with Gaudí, his architect. They believed in an alliance of business, new technology, religion and regional pride in order to create a new industrial society. With these ideals in mind, Eusebi Güell commissioned Gaudí to design a residential complex, far from the bustling city, a utopi-an enclave, uniting traditional Catalan culture with the modernity of the age of machinery. Under the architect's strict management, construction work on the park started in the year 1900 on Pelada mountain, what was formerly the outskirts of Barcelona. Due to the onset of the First World War and the bourgeoisie's lack of interest in the project, construction work ground to a definitive halt in 1914. Up until this time only the communal areas and two of the 60 houses planned had been built. Eventually, the park was used for parties, celebrations and conferences until it was acquired in 1922 by the Barcelona City Council to be transformed into a public park. In 1984 UNESCO declares it a World Heritage Site and from 1987 to 1994 it undergoes extensive restoration work.

Eusebi Güell
The park's promoter was an important textile industrialist who participated in the Catalan nationalist movement, was a Member of Parliament and named Count in 1910.

Original project
Gaudí developed a complete programme for the park.

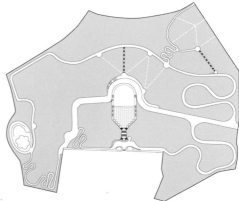

Gaudí's project

Built on the Pelada mountainside, this project designed by Gaudí set out to bring traditional Catalan values in line with the new industrial era.

Functionalism and symbolism

The garden city planned by Gaudí consisted of a park spanning 15 hectares, located on the slope of a rugged mountain. Surrounded by a wall with controlled entranceways, the park would possess communal areas, paths and walkways and 60 triangular private plots of land on which a house surrounded by a garden would be built. This project devised by Güell and Gaudí can be interpreted as a didactic programme aimed at reviving Catalan religious spirit. Using the high ground to his advantage, the architect devised the park as a pathway to spiritual elevation. In the lower section is the main entrance whose ornate lodges clearly alluded to the frivolities of the time and, on the higher level the chapel, the holy place, which would be reached by following the pathways as way of pilgrimage.

1900
IS THE YEAR in which work first commenced on the levelling out of land, the outer wall and the pathways.

Antoni Gaudí
When starting the park, he was also working on the construction of the Güell wine cellars, the Torre Bellesguard and the Sagrada Familia.

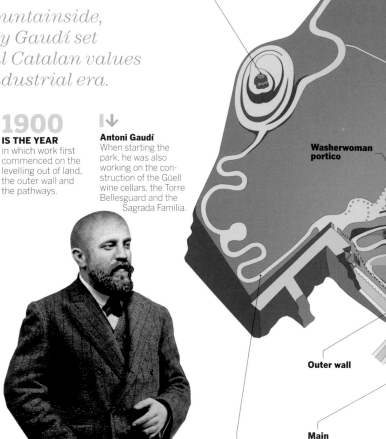

Calvary

Washerwoman portico

Outer wall

Pathway

Main entrance

DATA
GAUDÍ'S COLLABORATORS

During fourteen years of construction work on the park, Antoni Gaudí counted on the collaboration of a group of architects who completely shared his ideas: Joan Rubió, Francesc Berenguer, Llorenç Matamala, Josep Maria Jujol and Joan Bergós.

Joan Rubió

Francesc Berenguer

Llorenç Matamala

Josep Maria Jujol

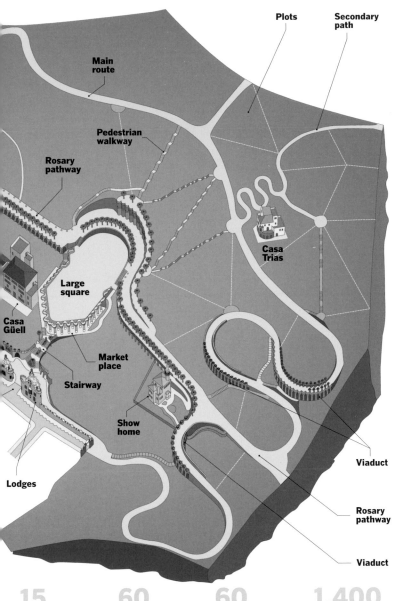

Plots

Secondary path

Main route

Pedestrian walkway

Rosary pathway

Casa Trias

Casa Güell

Large square

Market place

Stairway

Show home

Lodges

Viaduct

Rosary pathway

Viaduct

Sources of inspiration

The park is inspired by the youthful experiences and nationalist Catalan ideals of its promoter, Eusebi Güell. Thus, Gaudí used the *Jardín de la Fontaine* from the city of Nîmes as his inspiration, where Güell had studied in his youth and fondly recalled, when creating some of the constructions in the park. The park is also inspired by places in French and Spanish Catalonia and traditional Mediterranean constructions such as Greek and Egyptian temples. The architect managed to bring this array of influences together into a harmonious arrangement and by using nature as his guide evolved towards new architectonic solutions.

Undulating bench
It was the last work carried out in the park: it was finished in 1913 and Gaudí counted on architect Jujol's collaboration.

The stairway
The monumental stairway overcomes a drop of 8.10 metres and links the entrance with the central zone of the park.

15
HECTARES
is the total surface area of the land Eusebi Güell bought in order to make a garden city.

60
METRES
is the maximum height of the slope of the mountain on which the park is sited.

60
PLOTS
of triangular shape are planned for the construction of houses in the park.

1.400
METRES SQ
Is the average surface area of the plots created in the division of Park Güell.

02 | ENTRY TO THE PARK
The main entrance

Gaudí designed the park entrance as a great puzzle to decipher the ideals underlying the urbanization.

Antoni Gaudí planned the park's entrance with a double intention. On the one hand, to capture the public's attention and surprise with its fantastical constructions, as if they were stage scenery in an exotic theatrical work. On the other hand, to convey an allegorical message by means of numerous symbols and signs, in order that, like a mystery game, they could be interpreted by wise and ingenious people to achieve a higher plain of knowledge. Both intentions responded to the interests of a society that enjoyed the new and extravagant and who liked deciphering mysteries and riddles. During this period, the universal exhibitions held in large cities showed the latest industrial advances and set the trend for the exotic, which went hand in hand with the influence of new styles. Moreover, ingenuity became popular as a means of

unravelling the truth: popular theatre with puzzles and unexpected twists, detective tales and guessing games of intellectual café gatherings, were commonplace in Barcelona society. By putting together the symbolic pieces of the giant puzzle created by Gaudí for the park, like its location on the mountain, the circle generated by the wall, the gardens, the entranceway flanked by towers and the presence of exotic beasts such as the dragon and serpent, the main entrance to the Park Güell can be interpreted as an allegorical entranceway to paradise, paradise being a paradigm for the ideal enclave, Utopia. Thus from the very entrance of the park, the architect passes on the ideals and the general philosophy underlying this perfect community that would inhabit this gardened urbanization.

The outer wall
Built during the first years of the project, it was made of stone that was being extracted from the mountain. On the street called Olot, the wall measures 210 metres long and depending on the section ranges from 2 to 4 metres high.

The entrance to an ideal place

Vibrantly coloured and loaded with symbols and exotic forms, the entrance sets out to mark out the difference between the city outside and the ideal urbanization devised for Park Güell.

Side entrance
The park has a series of entrances that are placed along the length of its perimeter, which means that its residents don't only have to use the main entrance.

Access to the park

Gaudí positioned the main entrance to the park on the area of lower lying ground to facilitate access from the outside. The gate, executed in wrought iron, is covered in palm leaves and originally belonged to Casa Vicens but was brought to the park in 1965. It is flanked by two lodges of organic structure, which would be used for administration and maintenance purposes. These two lodges give rise to the wall that circles the park. Built with rustic stone extracted from the site, this wall is decorated with broken up ceramic tiles that alternate with circular medallions on which "Park" and "Güell" are inscribed. The wall, along with the lodges and the stairway, was constructed between 1900 and 1903.

5

4

3

1

Lodges
On either side of the entranceway are two striking lodges designed by Gaudí. One is used as the caretaker's lodge and the other by the park's administration.

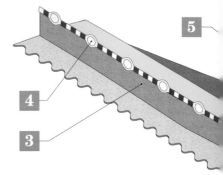

2

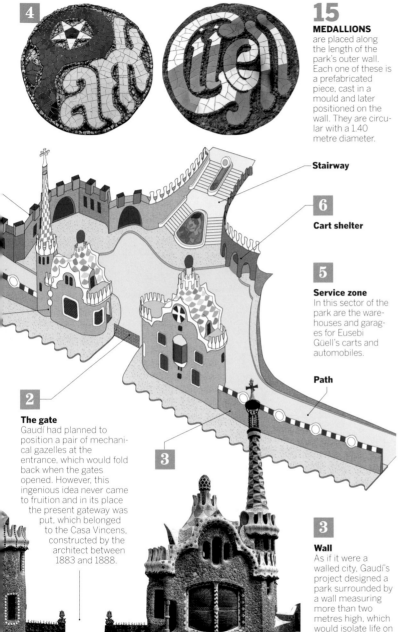

15
MEDALLIONS
are placed along the length of the park's outer wall. Each one of these is a prefabricated piece, cast in a mould and later positioned on the wall. They are circular with a 1.40 metre diameter.

Stairway

6

Cart shelter

5

Service zone
In this sector of the park are the warehouses and garages for Eusebi Güell's carts and automobiles.

Path

2

The gate
Gaudí had planned to position a pair of mechanical gazelles at the entrance, which would fold back when the gates opened. However, this ingenious idea never came to fruition and in its place the present gateway was put, which belonged to the Casa Vincens, constructed by the architect between 1883 and 1888.

3

Wall
As if it were a walled city, Gaudí's project designed a park surrounded by a wall measuring more than two metres high, which would isolate life on the inside from the hubbub of the outside world.

4

Medallions
The words "Park" and "Güell" alternately appear made of different coloured *trencadís*.

6

Cart shelter
Viewed from outside it resembles a walking elephant. Inside, it is like a cavern.

DATA
THE OTHER ENTRANCES

The park possesses six entrances; the main one is located on the street called Olot, two on either side of this one, at the start and the end of the street, two on the Avenida Coll del Portell and another on the Carretera del Carmel.

East entrance

The two lodges

Combining functionalism and aesthet-icism, Gaudí designed two monumen-tal lodges of organic, suggestive and evocative form at the main entrance.

Administration and caretaker's lodge

Despite their whimsical appearance, Gaudí rigorously designed the two entrance lodges and responded to the required functions with well-defined spaces. The smallest lodge, used for administration purposes, has two storeys, a small terrace and a tower topped by a four-armed cross, which soars 29 metres above ground level. In the past it had a telephone and seating for visitors. The largest lodge, with three floors, was used by the caretaker and had one room, a kitchen, various bedrooms, an attic and a small balcony. Both lodges are crowned by a mushroom-shaped cupola and combine rustic stone with bright ceramic *trencadís* work on the roofs.

The administration
It is the smallest of the two entrance lodges.

Prefabricated elements
When constructing the two lodges, Gaudí used various prefabricated pieces for the crenellations, the cupola terminations and eaves.

Trencadís detail

The tower
Measuring 17 metres high, the administration lodge tower is crowned by a four-armed cross pointing to the four cardinal points.

29
METRES
is the total distance from ground level to the cross, which adorns the administration lodge.

Tower detail
Gaudí used checkerboard *trencadís* work to decorate the tower's concave and convex forms.

The caretaker's entrance
It is reached by crossing a small area comprising of a column and two parabolic stone arches. The door is made of forged iron.

Fairytale house. The design of the lodges created by Gaudí resembles the house from the fairy tale of Hansel and Gretel.

21
METRES
is the distance
from the ground to
the top of the
cupola of the care-
taker's lodge.

Cupola
The cupola is dec-
orated with upside
down coffee cups.
It is said that, by
doing this Gaudí
gave up coffee.

**Caretaker's
lodge**
It is the largest of
the two entrance
lodges.

Inspiration

Due to their daring colours and attractive shapes, the entrance lodges have provoked many types of interpretations. Some considerations
point out that they could be fairy or
witches' castles or possibly two ele-
phants with seat saddles carrying
watchtowers. Other theories main-
tain that they are a result of psyche-
delic hallucinations brought about
by eating magic mushrooms. Sure-
ly, the most likely is that Gaudí was
inspired by the house made of can-
dy, sweets and caramels in the tale
of "Hansel and Gretel", which towards 1901 was being shown as an
opera in Barcelona and was trans-
lated into Catalan by Joan Maragall,
friend of Gaudí and Güell.

Window
The windows of the
two lodges are deco-
rated with ceramic
work of different col-
ours and designs.

Cupola
Mushroom-shaped,
the termination of
the cupola func-
tions as the lodge's
ventilation shaft.

Prefabricated
The cross on the win-
dow is made of the
same prefabricated
elements used for
the crenellations.

The innovation of the lodges

Gaudí managed to create surprising spaces by harmonizing the experimentation of new construction techniques with greater artistic freedom and unlimited creativity.

Technical innovations

Gaudí used the entrance lodges as a way of experimenting with new structural and constructive forms. The architect started to employ organic shapes and designed floors that had oval, sweeping perimeters with no corners nor right angles. For the ceilings, he worked with warped shapes and curves that evolved from straight lines. For the roofs he combined modern geometry with a traditional Catalan technique, the bricked vault technique, which consisted of cementing narrow bricks one on top of the other in order to achieve a fine and resistant structure. Moreover, he developed a system based on prefabricated modulation that consisted of manufacturing, with narrow brick, a series of pieces in the workshop and then transporting them to the place where they would be put into position to make up different parts of the lodges.

Administration lodge. Its design means that the interior is very bright.

1952
RESTORATION
After almost 50 years, the entrance lodges were repaired and their ceiling structure strengthened.

The four-armed cross
In 1936, at the start of the Civil War, the cross was destroyed and was replaced by a larger one. In the latter restoration it was returned to its original size.

DATA
THE INTERIOR

Two lodges, two different functions
The different spaces planned by Gaudí are designed with each one of the lodges' functions in mind, one as a dwelling for the caretaker's family and the other as reception and administration office.

Floor tile
The geometric design of tiles contrast with the lodges' organic forms.

01. The roof. Of organic shape, the roof of the caretaker's lodge is totally covered with vibrant *trencadís* work. **02. The window.** The openings planned by Gaudí delicately combine different materials, such as stone and ceramic work. **03. The window.** Situated in the administration lodge, it is one of the largest in the building. **04. The staircase.** The banister, made of wood and wrought iron, is clearly of Modernist inspiration. **05. The ceiling.** It is constructed with parallel beams that generate a pleasant sensation of movement.

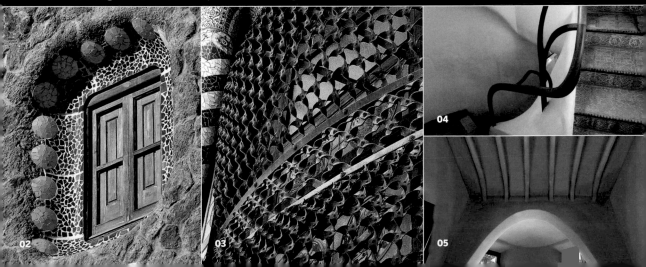

The park courtyard

Gaudí plans the transition space between the outside and inside as a large reception area that organises traffic flow to each and every corner of the park.

⊢→ Conical column
The column in the cart shelter is similar to the crypt of the Monastery of San Pere de Rodes, one of the most important Romanesque monasteries in Catalonia.

The park courtyard

Between the entrance lodges and the stairway is a space that Gaudí planned as the urbanization's reception area. A type of square that would act as organizer of the different routes leading to different areas in the park, with enough space, around 400 square metres that would enable various carts or automobiles to effortlessly manoeuvre. From this space the monumental stairway rises up to the hypostyle hall and towards the network of paths that cover the site. These types of reception areas were frequent in Gaudí's work, as can be appreciated in La Pedrera.

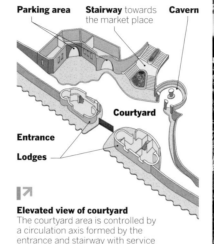

Parking area **Stairway** towards the market place **Cavern**

Courtyard

Entrance

Lodges

↗ Elevated view of courtyard
The courtyard area is controlled by a circulation axis formed by the entrance and stairway with service zones on either side.

|← The courtyard
Its surface area covers more than 400 square metres.

⋯? WHAT IS A CRENELLATION?
Each one of the teeth topping the walls of the old fortresses.

←

The service zone
Gaudí designed the parking and storage areas very near to the entrance so that these places could be easily accessed from the outside.

↙

Cart shelter
Like a cavern excavated out of stone, this space is of circular ground plan and its size means carts can easily enter and leave.

The service zone
Gaudí took advantage of the rugged terrain by placing two cavern-like excavated spaces built of rustic stone, which resemble medieval dungeons, on both sides of the stairway. Viewing the stairway face on, the left-hand space was for the warehouse and garage for Eusebi Güell's automobiles and carts. Whilst the other side, of completely circular ground plan, was used as a cart shelter on rainy or very hot days. This cavern is popularly known as "the elephant" given that, if one looks carefully, four legs, a stomach and trunk can be made out.

51
GAUDÍ'S AGE
when he finished building work on the main entrance of the park.

The shelter. It resembles a stone cavern.

↘ DATA
PREFABRICATED CRENELLATIONS

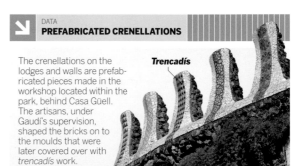

The crenellations on the lodges and walls are prefabricated pieces made in the workshop located within the park, behind Casa Güell. The artisans, under Gaudí's supervision, shaped the bricks on to the moulds that were later covered over with *trencadís* work.

Trencadís

03 | MEDITERRANEAN ESSENCE
Stairway and market place

Gaudí combined time-old Mediterranean traditions with the technical innovations of the period.

The architect wanted the route leading up to the upper section of the park to be spectacular. Therefore, a stairway of monumental proportions was planned along with a large hypostyle hall of Doric influence, popularly referred to as "the market place". These areas were built at different periods: between 1900 and 1903 the stairway was constructed and towards 1909 the colonnade was finished. As if it were the stage for a grand theatrical production, Gaudí bestowed it with iconic and symbolic sculptures, which were related to the ideals and concepts elaborated during the park's creation. Thus, many elements from Catalan geography and mythological themes can be made out, such as the cavern, the serpent, the dragon, the sun and the moon. The market's apparently simplistic and ancient appearance hides the new technical advances of the time. An ingenious system of iron beams supports the ceiling's perimeter, which in turn supports the undulating bench of the square above. Moreover, this entire area functions as a drainage system for the rainwater that flows down through the columns to the large cistern under the market place. This columned forest, inspired by Mediterranean heritage, harks back to classical Greek temples and was still built in spite of knowing the urbanization project would not prosper. Maybe in an attempt to profit from the investment, given that only three plots had been sold off, the park's promoter Eusebi Güell decided, towards 1913, to sell the medicinal spring water found in the rear part of the market place. Under the brand SARVA, the bottles were labelled with a photograph of the stairway and market place which read "Source: Park Güell (Neighbourhood of Health)".

➡

The dragon
Located on the third flight of the large stairway, the dragon or salamander, designed by Gaudí, has become the park's most popular and attractive sculpture.

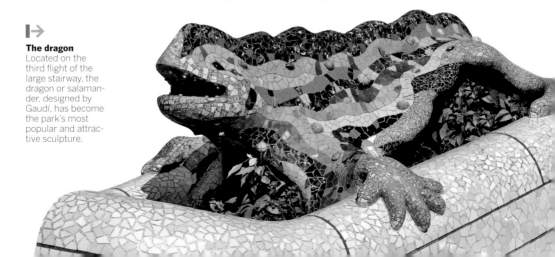

The stairway

With its 45 steps, the wide stairway is the first stage of the monumental circuit designed by Gaudí for the communal area of the urbanization.

The bench
When designing the bench on the fourth flight of stairs, Gaudí studied when it would be in the shade during summer and would receive sun during winter.

A monumental access way

Located between crenellated walls, the stairway leads up to the columned hall and is made up of three flights of eleven steps and one of twelve. The stairway is split in half by fountains with symbolic sculptures that as a whole represent the "Catalan countries": northern Catalonia, the French side and southern Catalonia, the Spanish side. On the fountain on the first flight, a circle represents the world and a graduated compass recalls Güell and Gaudí as promoter and architect of the park. On the second fountain, a shield with yellow and red bars constitutes the Catalan flag and a serpent on it alludes to medicine. On the third flight, the ceramic dragon is connected to the city of Nîmes, where Güell was educated. On the last flight is an odeon shaped bench.

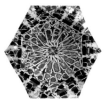

The hexagons
Found on the stairway, they resemble honeycomb cells. Perhaps Gaudí used them to symbolise work within the community.

2

2

The third fountain
Over a circular shaped basin is the tripod sculpture and, below, the popular dragon whose mouth trickles water which then flows down to the lower fountains like a waterfall.

3

The second fountain
Located on the second flight of steps, this fountain has a medallion shaped sculpture with hexagonal shield in its centre of the Catalan flag. Standing out is a serpent's head surrounded by ceramic incrustations resembling the fruit of the eucalyptus tree.

⊢→
The stairway
Divided in half by a group of fountains and sculptures, the stairway is completely symmetrical and measures 8.10 metres wide by 20 metres long.

45
STEPS
make up the monumental stairway, separated into four flights, one with 12 steps and the three other flights have 11 steps each.

8,10
METRES
is the drop between the courtyard and the market place, which Gaudí overcame with the stairway.

Second landing

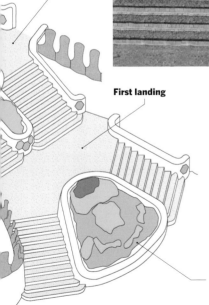

First landing

4

The first fountain
Between the naturalist elements is a graduated compass that alludes to Gaudí as architect.

⬎ DATA
DECORATION

On the lateral walls of the stairway, Gaudí intersperses prefabricated convex pieces of *trencadís* of varying colour and design with concave pieces of white *trencadís*. This arrangement of elements gives rise to a decorative wall of great artistic value.

The dragon

Vibrantly coloured and of gentle disposition, the dragon on the flight of steps has become Park Güell's and Gaudí's most popular sculpture.

The claw
Using *trencadís* technique meant that Gaudí could adapt the ceramic tile decoration accordingly to curved surfaces and create a rich and surprising aesthetic appearance.

An evocative figure

The dragon or salamander on the stairway is actually an overflow for the cistern located below the market place. It is a prefabricated piece that was made of hollow brick and later put into position to be then covered with ceramic tiles of vibrant colour. It used to boast sharper teeth and claws, but with time and restoration work this feature has been lost. It is said that Gaudí modelled the sculpture jumping on a metallic mesh until he achieved the desired effect. With time, this figure has become Park Güell's most emblematic sculpture and subject to many different interpretations and allusions: the mythological dragon Pythoness, protector of the subterranean waters of the temple of Delphi, an alchemic salamander representing fire or an interpretation of the French city of Nîmes' coat of arms where the park's promoter spent his youth.

Allusions
The dragon, along with the two palm trees flanking it, represents the city of Nîmes' coat of arms, where Güell was educated and which he fondly remembered.

Antoni Gaudí
In all his works, the architect would personally work on the concept and execution of the sculptures to obtain the aesthetic and symbolic value he required.

DATA
THE CERAMIC TRIPOD

On the upper part of the fountain rises a tripod-shaped sculpture that, according to various theories, might represent the Oracle of Delphi of the Sanctuary of Apollo, or the tail belonging to the serpent on the second fountain on the second flight of stairs.

The market place

Inspired by the temples of Ancient Greece, Gaudí planned a robust forest of columns of archaic style to shelter the urbanization's market place.

86
COLUMNS
make up the market place colonnade. They are fluted, of circular base, with a diameter of 1.20 metres, covered with *trencadís* and reach 1.80 metres high.

Mediterranean essence

Located on the second level of the park, the hypostyle hall monumentally rises over the stairway. Its construction was inspired in the Doric style of the Greek temples, which Gaudí modified by creating a more archaic appearance. According to the original project, this area was to be used as the market place for the community's inhabitants. The hall is made up of 86 columns measuring 6 metres high whose function is to support the weight of the square above. All of the columns are built with mortar and rubble, which resembles ancient marble, and the outer ones slightly tilt inwards for better structural balance. From one column to the other, the ceiling is covered with semi-spherical vaults covered with white *trencadís* and decorated with colourful ceiling rosettes.

The market place. It has 86 thick columns.

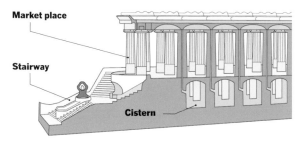

Market place

Stairway

Cistern

Cistern and market place
The underground cistern follows the same structure as the market place: an arrangement of columns set out equidistantly and united by vaults.

WHAT IS THE DORIC STYLE?
It is the oldest of the classical Greek architectonic styles. It is characterised by its robust proportions. The Parthenon on the Acropolis in Athens is its greatest exponent.

Gargoyle
On the cornice over the market place, there is a series of gargoyles, which represent lion heads, from whose gaping mouths rainwater drains.

The cistern

Below the market place, there is a large water tank with a 1.200 cubic metre capacity. This large deposit had to store the rainwater that would be used for irrigation and other community necessities. Its construction started in 1906 and was carried out in conjunction with the hypostyle market hall, which follows the same structure. Gaudí devised an ingenious drainage system that collected the rainwater that had fallen on to the square. Like a giant filter, the square's floor is made up of various layers of different sized stones, which means that the water can filter down without letting any soil pass through. Once the water is filtered, the semispherical vaults on the ceiling conduct it towards some pipes located within the columns, where it flows down to the underground cistern.

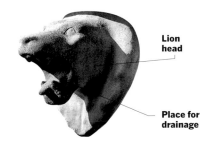

Lion head

Place for drainage

DATA
INSPIRED BY THE GREEKS

Gaudí interpreted the Doric style with a certain freedom and introduced some of his own elements such as the water droplets, which underline the large square's function as rainwater collector.

Stone droplets

Frieze with droplets of water

Suns and moons

In search of a new style, Gaudí and his collaborator, Jujol design the ceiling rosettes in the market place with broken pieces of tiles, bottles, plates and all kinds of everyday things.

The moon and sun

Jujol's ceiling rosettes

Gaudí decorates the ceiling vaults of the market place with lively coloured rosettes. Originally the hall could have had 90 columns, but the architect did away with four of them to put instead four ceiling rosettes, measuring three metres in diameter and, around them, three smaller ones measuring one metre in diameter. The largest ones represent the four seasons and share the same illustration, a twenty-pointed star, of different colours. The lunar cycle is depicted by the fourteen smaller ones, which are variations of swirls and spirals. The rosettes were executed by Gaudí's collaborator, the architect Jujol, and are comprised of broken pieces of ceramic work, bottles, cups, dolls and crockery, a technique that was later exploited by Cubists and Dadaists.

The ceiling. In the area on the ceiling where columns are omitted, Gaudí put the sun rosettes.

The hook
The sun rosettes have a hook that a lamp was hanged from.

4 SUNS
measuring three metres in diameter and of different colour decorate the market place ceiling.

14 MOONS
organised in groups of four are placed around the rosettes that represent the suns. The swirling and spiralling designs were done by architect Jujol.

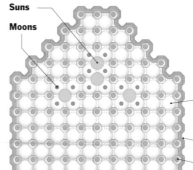

Suns

Moons

Surface area
The ceiling falls within a square of 43 by 43 metres, with a surface area of approximately 1.500 square metres.

Vaults
70 semi-spherical vaults cover the ceiling.

Frieze

Capitals
of the columns.

Ceiling layout. The striking rosettes occupy the central area of the market.

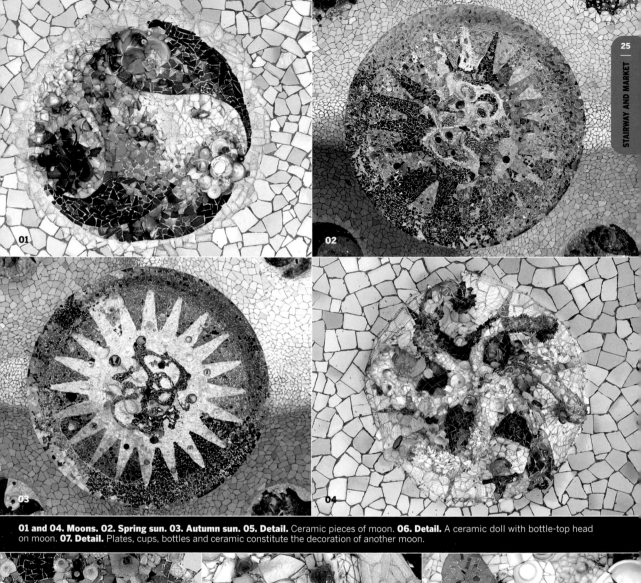

01 and 04. Moons. 02. Spring sun. 03. Autumn sun. 05. Detail. Ceramic pieces of moon. **06. Detail.** A ceramic doll with bottle-top head on moon. **07. Detail.** Plates, cups, bottles and ceramic constitute the decoration of another moon.

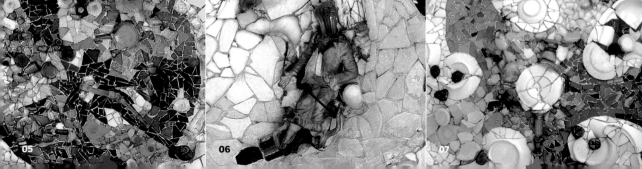

04 | A COMMUNAL AREA IN THE CENTRE OF THE PARK
The square and the bench

Gaudí rounded off work in the park with one of the most surprising artistic creations of the 20th century.

The large square was the last area to be built. Construction work on it commenced around 1907 along with the market place colonnade, which acted as its support, and in 1913, with the conclusion of the decoration on the undulating bench, it was judged as finished. At this moment, the park was deemed as practically complete, although work still continued on minor things up until 1914, coinciding with the start of the First World War. In the first plans of the park, Gaudí had named the large square as "Greek theatre" and as so referred to a great space on the mountainside that reminded of primitive Hellenic theatres. Güell and Gaudí were great admirers of Greek culture and classical theatre, as is illustrated in various works of the architect, where he included spaces designed for the same use. But, with Park Güell, the function of the large square was not only intended as a theatre for entertainment, but was also created as a ceremonial and communal nucleus for civic, social and religious meetings. With this in mind, Gaudí placed the large square in the geographical centre of the park, transforming it into a strategic point, easily accessed from any area in the park, and symbolic, given that it emphasizes the importance of community life within a utopian urbanization. The architect's aspirations were only partly carried out, given that this area, over time, was used for less formal ends, like popular dance festivals or bicycle races, but very few religious acts and theatrical works.

**The square
and the bench**
With a surface area of more than 3.000 square metres, the large square is the widest space in the park. A part of it is excavated out from the mountainside and the other part, delimited by the undulating bench, is over the market place.

The large square

In the central zone of the park, Gaudí designs a large space in the form of a Greek theatre that was destined to be the heart of community life in the urbanization.

The communal area

Devised by Gaudí as nucleus of community life, the large square was planned as the meeting point of the urbanization and ceremonial area, where civil and religious celebrations would take place. Situated in the park's geographical centre, it is 86 metres long by 43 metres wide and its oval shape resembles an ancient Greek theatre that could be found in Athens or Delphi. The rear part of the square is dug out from the mountainside and functions as a great natural amphitheatre. On the opposite side, situated over the market place, is the marvellous undulating serpentine bench that commands panoramic views of Barcelona.

1907

WORK COMMENCES

The large square was started around 1907 along with the market colonnade. When work was concluded on the undulating bench towards 1913, the central area in the park was complete.

The square today

The large square in the park has become a great viewing platform that the city of Barcelona and the Mediterranean can be observed from.

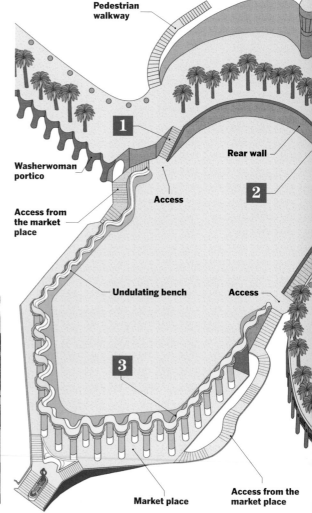

Pedestrian walkway

Washerwoman portico

1

Rear wall

Access

2

Access from the market place

Undulating bench

Access

3

Market place

Access from the market place

Car show
Amongst the varying activities that took place in the large square, in 1908 a car show was put on, demonstrating different makes and models of automobiles.

Rosary pathway

The people's square
Since its inauguration, around 1909, its use has been less formal than Gaudí had intended. The large square has played host to the *"sardana"*, the Catalan national dance, some Red Cross charity events with great processions of military bands, launching of balloons, bicycle races and even an automobile show. Paradoxically, only a few theatrical productions were staged.

Antoni Gaudí
In 1909, the architect designed an arrangement of terraced stands for the large square for the theatrical production of *King Oedipus*, but due to the social unrest of *La Semana Trágica* the work was cancelled and never put on in the end.

 Access
The square has two entrances, one on either side, halfway up, which connect it with the market and the Rosary pathway.

 Rear part
The rear part of the square is excavated in the mountainside and decorated with palm trees.

 Undulating bench
The part of the square that is over the market place is decorated with a bench that functions as railing.

The undulating bench

Gaudí wanted maximum functionalism for a bench that, ahead of the artistic vanguards of the time, would become one of the greatest works of 20th century art.

A work ahead of its time

The bench, which borders half the square, was one of the last works carried out in the park. It was started in 1909 above the market place, as a crowning piece, and had to fulfil various functions simultaneously, such as square balustrade, balcony-view-point, bench for visitors as well as a drainage system for rainwater. By combining aestheticism and functionalism, Gaudí devised a striking work that has generated a multitude of interpretations, from mythological serpents and dragons to the waves in the sea. The bench, a blend of sculpture and abstract collage, is considered to be at the forefront of cubist and surrealist aestheticism.

The undulations
By alternating concave and convex modules, Gaudí endows the bench with wider and more closed undulations that create spaces similar to theatre boxes.

Ergonomics
Gaudí designed the bench to perfectly adapt to the human form.

Sequence of concave and convex modules

White *trencadís*

Exterior view of bench
The outer decoration of the bench is made up of a large variety of figurative images, whilst on the inside it is colourful and totally abstract.

Functionalism

In search of maximum functionalism, Gaudí carried out an ergonomic study to find the most comfortable form of seating for the user. He therefore counted on the assistance of one of the park workers, who tried out the bench and acted as model. At the same time, the architect wanted the serpentine bench to fit in with the community functions of the large square; such as recreation area and place of cultural acts, festivals and shows. This is how Gaudí developed a module comprised of various parts, which he then repeated to create the bench's continuous undulations. This method enabled him to create more reduced areas where people could gather in the intimacy of small groups and more open areas for larger groups.

Sagittarius sign of the zodiac

Pisces sign of the zodiac

Cancer sign of the zodiac

Aries sign of the zodiac

110
METRES
is the approximate length of the entire bench, maybe one of the longest artistic works in the world.

— **Drain**
The backrests of the modules have a hole that rainwater falling on to the seat drains down.

DATA
THE BENCH MODULATION

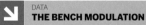

In order to build the bench, Gaudí developed one segment measuring one and a half metres and two back rests that were combined in such a way that they created the incoming and outgoing curves desired by the architect. The modules were built with bricks in another area of the park and were later joined together in the corresponding place.

1 Convex module

2 Concave module

3 Joins
The bench is made up of concave and convex modules.

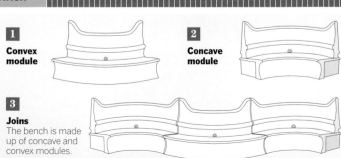

Trencadís

Broken up ceramic pieces, tiles, bottles and even pieces of his own crockery were used by the architect Jujol for the surprising decoration of Gaudí's undulating bench.

Josep Maria Jujol
Gaudí had full confidence in his collaborator and allowed him total freedom when decorating the inside of the undulating bench.

Art and technique

Regarding the decoration of the undulating bench, Gaudí counted on the collaboration of architect Jujol, who used tiles and broken crockery. Apparently, Gaudí and Jujol gave the labourers free reign to decorate in the style of a large collage, but on the condition that they respected certain guidelines, so that a magnificent superposition of colours and textures would be created. On the outer decoration of the bench images of palm trees with five branches abound, representations of the zodiac signs, stars and organic forms. On the inside part, on the backrest, the colours mix in an abstract way, blue, green and yellow tones predominate, which for Gaudí, symbolised Faith, Hope and Charity. Jujol also included a large quantity of elements that paid homage to the Virgin Mary, such as roses and allegorical phrases.

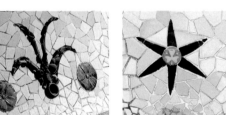

Details on the bench exterior
Between the drainage holes, the bench has different figurative designs and organic marine-like forms. Six-pointed starfish, varying fish, crabs and twisting seaweed mixed with flowers and clovers can be found here.

WHAT IS *TRENCADÍS*?
It is a technique that consists of using irregular fragments of ceramic work or other materials to cover a surface.

DATA
MESSAGES ON THE CERAMIC WORK

On the backs of the bench, the ceramic pieces in the shape of semi-circular moulds, which form a continuous line, were specially made. Before they were baked, Josep Maria Jujol scratched some drawings and inscriptions on to some pieces with simple Marian invocations.

05 | AN EASILY ACCESSIBLE URBANIZATION
The pathways in the park

Gaudí planned innovative solutions to get over the terrain's rough and uneven topography.

When commencing the project around 1900, Gaudí set about solving the great irregularities of the land, more than 60 metres, and thus provide greater accessibility to different corners of the park. Therefore and in the space of just two years, he created an ingenious and complex system of main and secondary thoroughfares for carts and automobiles as well as shortcuts for pedestrians, which became the fundamental framework of the future garden city. The three kilometres of winding paths, some of them like arched viaducts, were adapted to the rugged land and spirally climb the mountain, surrounded by carob trees, pines and dense, rustic vegetation. To link up the steeper areas, the architect planned a series of ingenious bridges that were only built with materials originating from the quarries of the same park. Also, to improve pedestrian access, he planned narrow, steep and stepped pathways that were to be used as shortcuts. Gaudí, also inspired by the age-old tradition of pilgrimage, a very popular activity in the period, put many elements associated to religion that typify Catalan landscape along Park Güell's paths, such as caverns, cloisters, rosaries and sanctuaries. In a symbolic plan, the architect planned a circuit that climbed up winding paths, a spiritual ascension towards the highest area in the park leading up to where the chapel would be, although only the Calvary was constructed in the end.

▮→
Viaducts
The three viaducts for the vehicles, designed by Gaudí, emerge below arched pathways that shelter passers-by from sun and rain.

The Washerwoman portico

Gaudí proposes innovative solutions by blending the columns, ceilings and walls of the portico into just one continuous fluid and organic structure.

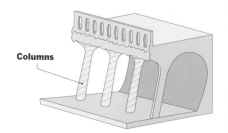

Columns

Towards organic architecture

The portico goes around Casa Güell and is comprised of two different stretches. The first takes the shape of a Romanesque cloister and has a series of double columns: the inside ones leaning inwards in order to support the weight of the soil and the outer columns are like palm trees of varying decorations except the one representing a washerwoman, which the portico gets its name from. The second stretch of the portico is a spiralling ramp, whose columns follow a helicoidal movement. Gaudí plans that the columns, ceiling and walls are joined in a fluid way, in the shape of a large wave in the ocean. In this way nature shows the architect how to develop new structural solutions.

Columns. One of the columns represents a washerwoman.

Stone. It is the main element.

WHAT IS A PORTICO?
It is an arched or columned gallery along the wall of a façade or patio.

The design game
The types of columns are all different and each one of them is covered in rustic stone.

Palm tree shaped

01

01. Second stretch of portico. In some places, because of the uneven land, a double level of helicoidal columns was made, tilted in order to support the weight of the soil better. **02. The capital.** On some of the portico columns, Gaudí planned palm tree shaped sculptures. **03. The door.** Situated at the start of the Washerwoman portico, it is worked in wrought iron. **04. Helicoidal columns.** Gaudí used the helicoidal shape for some of the columns to withstand the weight of the soil better.

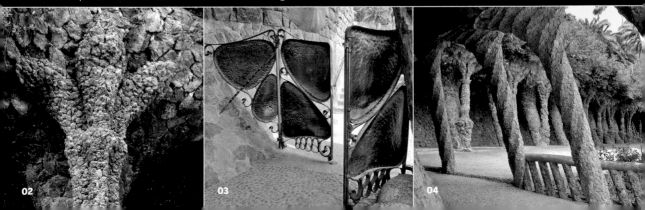

02

03

04

The viaducts

Decorated with rustic stone extracted from the very same place, Gaudí designs the viaducts in such a way that they perfectly blend into the park's natural surroundings.

The benches
The upper viaduct has benches attached to columns that, by being in the shade, make a relaxing resting area.

The viaduct system

The pathway that climbs up to the upper section of the park has three arched viaducts built by Gaudí to get round the ravines and the rugged topography of the land. Each viaduct has it own and particular character, although all combine technical innovations with an ancient and rustic appearance. They are built with brick and covered over in stone extracted from the park, generating spaces reminiscent of traditional places from Catalan geography, like mountain sanctuaries, cloisters and caverns. The lower viaduct has two rows of tilted columns and in the upper part are flowerbeds and benches. The midway viaduct has three rows of columns with the outer ones leaning like the upper viaduct. The latter has stone benches on the base and flowerbeds high up on the pillars.

Midway viaduct
It has three rows of thick columns with tilted outer ones. The interior walkway is home to a carob tree that Gaudí decided to keep as it was there before the portico was built.

Midway viaduct
The columns support the main route leading to the Calvary, just like the other viaducts do.

Lower viaduct
It is made up of two rows of inwardly tilting columns.

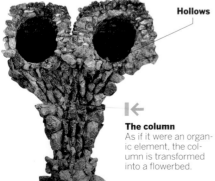

Hollows

The column
As if it were an organic element, the column is transformed into a flowerbed.

The flowerbed
Of large size, rising 2.80 metres high and home to an agave plant.

Upper viaduct
Along the way are raised flower-beds and stone benches.

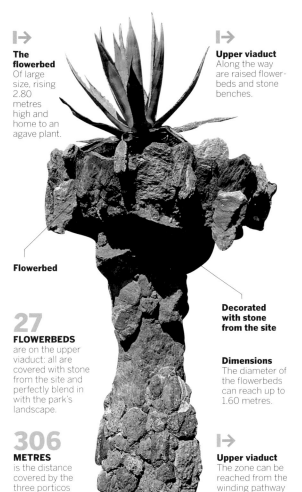

Flowerbed

Decorated with stone from the site

27
FLOWERBEDS
are on the upper viaduct: all are covered with stone from the site and perfectly blend in with the park's landscape.

Dimensions
The diameter of the flowerbeds can reach up to 1.60 metres.

306
METRES
is the distance covered by the three porticos built for the park pathways.

Upper viaduct
The zone can be reached from the winding pathway by means of a flight of steps.

 DATA
THE THREE MODELS

Despite carrying out similar functions and sharing the same structural concept, the three porticos designed by Gaudí present different aesthetic solutions and different histori-cal styles are alluded to: Gothic on the lower viaduct, Baroque on the midway one and Romanesque on the upper one.

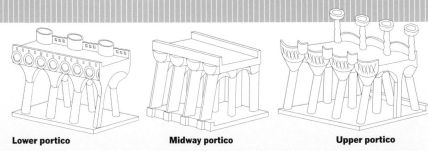

Lower portico   **Midway portico**   **Upper portico**

The Calvary

The discovery of prehistoric caves in the area that was destined for the chapel inspired Gaudí to build the Calvary in the shape of a rustic stone massif of megalithic appearance.

The crosses
All three are different and point in varying directions. The central and highest one is Jesus' cross, the smallest one has a triangular ending that resembles an arrow.

A megalithic monument

As a metaphor of spiritual elevation, Gaudí planned a chapel on Mount Menas, the highest area in the park. Due to the failure of the project of the park the chapel was never built, but a Calvary of circular ground plan was put instead, with two flights of steps leading up to its summit where three stone crosses are found. When commencing building work they came across prehistoric caves holding rhinoceros and other animal fossils and, perhaps, this discovery inspired the architect to build a monument inspired by the megalithic talayots of the Balearic Isles and in this way, confer an ancestral past on the park and Catalonia.

Ground plan
It is circular with steps on both sides.

1936

THE CROSSES ARE DESTROYED

The present crosses are not the original ones, as they were destroyed during the Civil War.

The three crosses

...?

WHAT IS A TALAYOT?

It is a prehistoric monument from the Balearic Isles, similar to a low tower. It is believed to have had a religious ceremonial purpose.

The cave
Below the monument is a cave, which was bricked up in 1960 to avoid accidents.

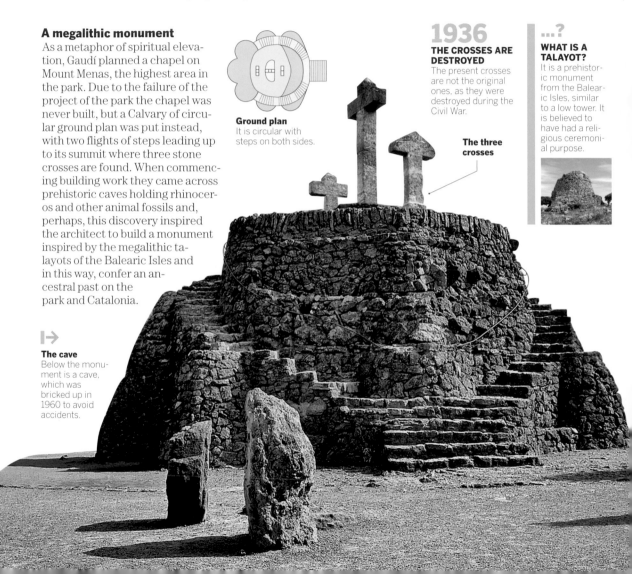

01. The Calvary. It is located on the west side of the park, on top of Mount Menas. A talayot with three crosses is found here and Gaudí wanted to build it on one of the highest areas of the park. **02. The crosses.** Made from rustic stone, they are located on top of the talayot and can be seen from far away. **03. The steps.** The steps going round this megalithic style structure were built entirely with stones taken from the park. **04. Barcelona at its feet.** The Calvary commands some magnificent views of the city.

06 | The Gaudí House Museum

Gaudí resided in Park Güell in the modernist villa built as show-home for the urbanization.

The house that Antoni Gaudí lived in for around twenty years was constructed between 1903 and 1904 by his collaborator Francesc Berenguer and was used as a show-home for prospective property owners of the urbanization. Towards 1906 and due to the lack of interest shown in Park Güell, Gaudí decided to purchase the villa as the park's surroundings and good atmosphere lent ideal conditions for the welfare of his ill father. Halfway through the same year, he moved into the villa with his orphaned niece Rosita, the maid and his father Francesc, who then died a few months later. The house, which Gaudí had to mortgage for not having enough money, was known as the *pink tower* and was lived in until 1925, when Gaudí went to live in his workshop-studio in the Sagrada Familia temple. A short time afterwards, on the 7th of June

1926, Gaudí is run over by a tram and in his will he leaves the villa to the Construction Committee of Sagrada Familia who, needing funds to carry on with the work, puts it up for sale. One year later, an Italian couple purchase it, Francesc Chiappo Arietti and his wife. The Chiappo couple lived various years in the villa in the park and as they had no children they left it to a nephew and, on his death; the new heirs offered it to the *Amigos de Gaudí* association. In the year 1960, the latter acquires it with the aim of converting it into a museum dedicated to Antoni Gaudí, and recreates how the architect's surroundings were when residing there. In 1963 it is officially inaugurated and in 1992, the association decides to transfer control of the Gaudí House Museum back to the Construction Committee of the Temple of the Sagrada Familia.

The Batlló chair
The museum holds pieces of furniture especially designed by Gaudí for his works, including the chair created for Casa Batlló.

The Calvet chair
It is one of the first pieces of furniture of anatomical design that Gaudí created.

The house where Gaudí resided

In 1906 Gaudí purchases the villa in the park and lives there for twenty years, during which there are only other two neighbours: Eusebi Güell, the park's promoter and the Trias family.

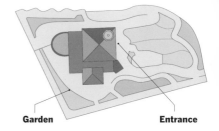

Garden   **Entrance**

Berenguer's project

The building planned by Gaudí's collaborator, architect Francesc Berenguer, is along side the Rosary pathway. It was constructed on rugged terrain and surrounded by a spacious garden with native and wild plants, according to Gaudí's preferences. The villa has three storeys, two spacious terraces, a basement with a cave found on the site and a tower topped by a cross and weather vane. Apart from having wide spaces and various rooms, it was equipped with the home comforts of the period such as electric lighting and hot water. The house's decoration, like the front wrought iron balustrade, the chimneys, tower decorated with coloured *trencadís* or the iron pergola in the garden all show Gaudí's direct influence.

I→

The House Museum
The villa designed by Francesc Berenguer is surrounded by a low wall and a rustic garden.

I←

The cross
In the garden are various elements designed by Gaudí for his works, such as the four-armed cross for the entrance of the Miralles property.

1906

GAUDÍ BUYS
the villa that is used as show-home for potential buyers and moves in with his father, his niece and the maid.

I→

Smoke vent
IInspired by the organic growth of mushrooms, the two chimneys on the house are decorated with coloured ceramic *trencadís*.

Sgrafitti
The exterior of the house is decorated in modernist style with drawings, of curved and spiralling form, sgrafittied on to the walls.

WHAT IS SGRAFITTI?
It is a drawing technique that consists of scratching the plaster surface on the wall to reveal a layer underneath. It was commonly used by modernist architects.

The windows
The villa has numerous windows; all are decorated with curving forms.

The "M" of Mary
The entrance of the villa is presided over by a letter "M" that is sgraffittied on the doorway and surrounded by twelve stars, which refer to the Virgin Mary.

The iron gates. The entrance is located on the Rosary pathway, the main thoroughfare of the park.

DATA
DISTRIBUTION

Gaudí's helper, Francesc Berenguer, was in charge of working on the project of the house. Its distribution, sober and functional meant all rooms would receive ventilation and natural light.

First floor

Second floor

The museum and its exhibits

In 1960, the association "Amigos de Gaudí" buys the villa where the architect lived and converts it into a magnificent House Museum.

20
YEARS
Gaudí lived in the house in Park Güell for twenty years, from 1906 until he moved into his work-shop in the Temple of La Sagrada Famil-ia in 1925.

Gaudí's legacy

The museum has three floors ex-hibiting objects and furniture be-longing to the architect and his closest collaborators. On the first floor is the Batlló room, with a set of chairs and a dining table de-signed by Gaudí for Casa Batlló on Passeig de Gràcia and the Calvet room exhibits furniture designed by the architect for Casa Calvet's lounge. On the second floor is Gaudí's study, his bedroom with a modernist style iron bedstead, the Güell-Jujol-Berenguer room, which holds pieces and items re-lating to Gaudí's three friends, the Ibarz-Clapés room and the Milà room, where some wooden cup-boards can be seen along with the hydraulic tiled flooring originat-ing from La Pedrera. In the base-ment is the Maní room, which ex-hibits the work of this artist that collaborated with Gaudí.

I←

The hall
It is the main hallway of the house and from this point many differ-ent parts of the muse-um can be accessed.

1963
IS WHEN THE HOUSE
is inaugurated as museum, exhibiting furniture designed by Gaudí and pieces by collaborating artists.

The ceilings. Some were decorated.

I←

Wrought iron lamp
In the Güell room, on the sec-ond floor, there is a ceiling light of modernist style, designed by Gaudí's collabo-rator, Francesc Berenguer.

I←

A sculpture of Gaudí
In the hall on the first floor, there is a bronze bust carried out by one of Gaudí's collabo-rators, sculptor Joan Matamala i Flotats.

I←

La Pedrera altarpiece
In Gaudí's bed-room, located on the second floor, is a piece designed in wood and stuccoed ivory for Casa Milà, by sculptor Josep Llimona.